THE WONDERS OF CANADA
EXPLORING CANADA
Lynda Sorensen

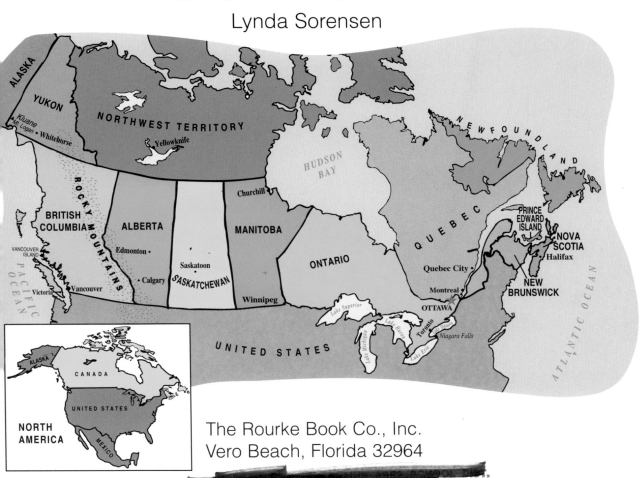

The Rourke Book Co., Inc.
Vero Beach, Florida 32964

Edited by Sandra A. Robinson and
Pamela J.P. Schroeder

PHOTO CREDITS
© Lynn M. Stone: cover, pages 4, 7, 12, 15, 17; © Thomas
Kitchin: pages 8, 10, 21; © Jerry Hennen: page 13; © Tom and
Pat Leeson: page 18

Library of Congress Cataloging-in-Publication Data

Sorensen, Lynda, 1953-
    The wonders of Canada / by Lynda Sorensen.
    p. cm. — (Exploring Canada)
    Includes index.
    ISBN 1-55916-103-5
    1. Canada—Description and travel—Juvenile literature.
2. Natural history—Canada—Juvenile literature. I. Title. II. Series.
F1017.S67   1995
917.1—dc20   94-48247
                                                             CIP
                                                             AC

Printed in the USA

TABLE OF CONTENTS

THE WONDERS OF CANADA

Canada's natural wonders are as plentiful as its golden autumn leaves. People can find Canada's wonders in every corner of the country, from the Pacific Coast to the Atlantic.

Many of these wonders, from waterfalls to tall mountains and deep canyons, are protected in parks. Canada has more than 35 national parks. Also, the 10 **provinces** and two **territories** in Canada have nearly 1,500 parks of their own.

National and provincial parks protect much of Canada's natural beauty, like these snowy mountains in Jasper National Park

THE BAY OF FUNDY

The Bay of Fundy lies between Nova Scotia and New Brunswick in eastern Canada.

It has the highest ocean **tides** in the world! Miles of mud flats appear during low tide in the bay. The mud flats disappear quickly, though, under waves of seawater when high tide rolls in.

The ocean level in the bay can be 50 feet (15 meters) higher at high tide than at low tide. In most parts of the world, high tide is only two or three feet (1 meter) higher than low tide.

Low tide along the shore of Kent Island in the Bay of Fundy reveals great pastures of seaweed

NIAGARA FALLS

The noise from tons of water falling 180 feet (55 meters) is deafening! The mist is drenching! The view is stunning!

This is Niagara Falls, which is actually two great waterfalls in two countries.

The falls—American Falls and Canadian Falls— plunge downward together from the Niagara River between Ontario and New York. The Canadian, or Horseshoe Falls are much wider, stretching 2,600 feet (792 meters) across. The best view of the falls is from the Ontario side.

Canadian (Horseshoe) Falls
plunge 180 feet (55 meters)

THE GREAT LAKES

The Great Lakes are huge bodies of fresh water that lie between Canada and the United States. Four of the Great Lakes—Superior, Huron, Erie and Ontario—are shared by the two countries.

These lakes are among the 12 largest freshwater lakes anywhere. Lake Superior is the largest in the world!

Several of Canada's national and provincial parks are along the lakeshores.

Sibley Provincial Park in Ontario reaches into the deep, dark blue water of Lake Superior

A young Dall sheep views the mountain wilderness of Kluane National Park

*A canoe floats on the quiet surface of Moraine Lake
in Banff National Park, Alberta*

THE NORTHERN ROCKIES

The mighty Rocky Mountains form the spine of North America. The Canadian, or northern Rockies reach from southern Alberta north into the Yukon.

Several national parks, such as Banff and Jasper, help protect the wonders of the Rockies for everyone.

In the high country of the Rockies are snow-capped peaks, forests, blue lakes and thousands of **glaciers.** Mountain rivers tumble into deep valleys.

Grizzly bears, wolves, mountain lions, elk and many other mountain animals live in the Rockies.

The northern Rockies are the backbone of western Canada

THE CANADIAN ARCTIC

One of Canada's least-known wonders is its Arctic country in the Far North.

The Far North is a treeless wilderness of open **tundra,** icy shores and snowy mountains. It is a land almost without any roads or people.

During the summer, the Arctic warms with 24 hours of sunlight each day. Wild animals gather in great numbers—including thousands of caribou, birds, wolves and other creatures.

The summer sun sets just before midnight on a lake in the Canadian tundra

THE POLAR BEARS OF CHURCHILL

Churchill, Manitoba, is just a little town on the shore of cold Hudson Bay. However, it gets a little bigger every fall when visitors arrive to watch the polar bears.

Dozens of polar bears travel through the Churchill area each fall, and Churchill earns its nickname—"Polar Bear Capital of the World."

Having a town along their path doesn't seem to bother the bears. They usually stay out of Churchill itself. When Hudson Bay freezes in late November, the bears hike far out onto the ice.

Polar bears wrestle near Churchill, Manitoba, before hiking onto the winter ice of Hudson Bay

THE GASPÉ PENINSULA

The scenic Gaspé Peninsula of Quebec reaches 150 miles (242 kilometers) into the sea, like a bent thumb.

Seaside villages share the shoreline with rocky cliffs, sandy beaches and forests. Mount Jacques Cartier is the peninsula's highest peak at 4,160 feet (1,268 meters).

The hills and woodlands of Forillon National Park cover the tip of the Gaspé Peninsula. Bonaventure Island, a protected home for 35,000 nesting **gannets,** lies offshore.

Percé Rock is a famous natural landmark at the end of the Gaspé Peninsula

KLUANE

Kluane (kloo AH nee) is a magnificent wilderness in the Yukon Territory. Much of the Kluane region's beauty lies within Kluane National Park—Canada's second-largest national park.

Mount Logan, Canada's tallest peak, towers above Kluane's hidden lakes, forests and more than 4,000 glaciers! Most of Kluane's wonders are in **remote** back country. Only hikers can reach them.

About 250 grizzly bears and several hundred Dall sheep live in this mountain park.

Glossary

gannet (GAH net) — a large, white, sharp-billed sea bird of the North Atlantic

glacier (GLAY shur) — a massive river of ice

province (PRAH vints) — any one of the 10 statelike regions, which together with the two territories, make up Canada

remote (ree MOTE) — somewhere far away or out-of-the-way

territory (TARE uh tor ee) — either of Canada's two northern regions, which together with the 10 provinces, make up Canada

tide (TIDE) — the rise and fall of water levels in the oceans, caused by the moon's gravity, or pull

tundra (TUN druh) — the treeless carpet of low-lying plants in the Far North and on mountains above the tree line

INDEX